Major Books by James DeMeo, PhD

* *Saharasia: The 4000 BCE Origins of Child Abuse, Sex-Repression, Warfare and Social Violence In the Deserts of the Old World,* Revised Second Edition, 2006

* *Preliminary Analysis of Changes in Kansas Weather Coincidental to Experimental Operations with a Reich Cloudbuster: From a 1979 Research Project,* 2010

* *In Defense of Wilhelm Reich: Opposing the 80-Year War of Mainstream Defamatory Slander Against One of the 20th Century's Most Brilliant Physicians and Natural Scientists,* 2013

* *The Orgone Accumulator Handbook: Wilhelm Reich's Life-Energy Discoveries and Healing Tools for the 21st Century, with Construction Plans,* 2010

* (Editor) *Heretic's Notebook: Emotions, Protocells, Ether-Drift and Cosmic Life-Energy, with New Research Supporting Wilhelm Reich,* 2002

* (Editor) *On Wilhelm Reich and Orgonomy,* 1993

* (Editor, with Bernd Senf) *Nach Reich: Neue Forschungen zur Orgonomie: Sexualökonomie, Die Entdeckung der Orgonenergie,* 1997

Marx Engels Lenin Trotsky: Genocide Quotes

The Hidden History of Communism's Founding Tyrants, in their Own Words

by

James DeMeo, PhD

Natural Energy Works
Ashland, Oregon, USA
www.naturalenergyworks.net

Publication and worldwide distribution rights:

Natural Energy Works
PO Box 1148
Ashland, Oregon 97520
United States of America
http://www.naturalenergyworks.net

Email: info@naturalenergyworks.net

Also available through Lightning Source / Ingram Distribution

ISBN: 978-0-9974057-0-5   0-9974057-0-8

First Edition, 2016

160422

Cover colors and textures are reproduced from a well-worn copy of Mao Zedong's original *Little Red Book*. The front cover image of Marx, Engels and Lenin is the author's photo of a tapestry hanging on a wall in the *Stasi Museum* in Berlin, Germany. By the time this tapestry had been made, Trotsky had been murdered and excommunicated from Communist Sainthood, his image erased from public display.

Hidden History of Communism's Founding Tyrants

CONTENTS

The Four Horsemen of the Communist Apocalypse

Introduction

Josef Stalin and Mao Zedong were cruel totalitarian butchers, who together with other Communist leaders and their followers, murdered nearly 100 million people over the 20th Century.§ While most admirers of Marxist Socialism and Communism accept those facts, they often complain: *"Stalin and Mao betrayed the original Communism of Marx and Engels!"* Or, *"Lenin freed the Russian People and if Trotsky had won the power struggle with Stalin, things would have gone differently!"* So say the Marxists. However, a dispassionate examination of the lesser-known writings of Communism's Founding Tyrants, things they wrote in obscure books, articles, letters, documents, briefs and telegrams, indicate this benign view *simply isn't true.*

Comrades Marx and Engels advocated war, slavery, racism, ethnic hatred and genocide. They mocked justice, freedom, democracy and equality, and had only contempt for the poor, workers, farmers and moderates. They slandered Jews as back-stabbing money-grubbers and spoke positively about black slavery, frequently using the term "nigger".

Comrades Lenin and Trotsky later put Marx & Engels into practice, instituting a reign of terror, assassinations, slavery, mass-murder and genocide. They promised democracy but usurped it, imprisoning or murdering dissenters, opponents and "counter-revolutionaries." They seized food from starving farmers, executed surrendered and wounded soldiers, along with prostitutes, alcoholics, peasants, factory workers, tradesmen, villagers and entire ethnic groups, with mass deportations of men, women and children, old and young, off to the Siberian Gulag which they, and not Stalin, originally created.

Within the unreformed autocratic Empires of Europe – notably in Tsarist Russia – the ideas of Marx and Engels were eagerly

---

§ Courtois, S., et al.: *The Black Book of Communism: Crimes, Terror, Repression*, Harvard U. Press, 1999 devoured by late 19th and early 20th Century reformers and revolutionaries. Their violent ideology resonated with the emotional dynamics of the times, the great longing for freedom mixed with fury and revenge-seeking. Marxist Socialism and Communism promised quick and decisive Revolution, with democracy, freedoms and a "workers paradise", but factually delivered dictatorial rule by self-appointed Marxist killers, father-figure "elites" supported by death-squad pistoleros who would sweep aside all who stood in their way. They held in contempt any and all efforts towards more gradual or authentically democratic social reforms, and as history shows, those individuals who supported Communism with the greatest passion quite eagerly, and hungrily, took up the gun. Assassinations and murdering of political oppositionists quickly followed, eventually and predictably including the murder of fellow revolutionaries, on the bloody road to creation of a desired utopian "dictatorship of the proletariat", the "ideal State".

As history shows, every nation that followed the Pied Piper of Marx and Engels, or later of Lenin, Trotsky, Stalin and Mao, unwaveringly descended into the conditions of prison Hell-states, and bloodbaths of *democide* – the murder of citizens by their own governments. Texts and biographies on Stalin and Mao abound, and expose their genocidal sentiments and actions in great detail. However, only a smaller amount has been written to directly expose the similar bloody sentiments of Communism's founding tyrants: Marx, Engels, Lenin and Trotsky.

Two primary works of Marx and Engels provided a backbone for their dictatorial movements. *The Communist Manifesto*, written by Marx and Engels in 1848, was a short work which outlined the general theory and principles by which international Communist societies would be formed and regulated. The first volume of Marx's more detailed exposition of Communism, *Das Kapital,* appeared in 1867, with more definitive editions appearing in 1885 and 1894, only after Marx's death, and being cobbled together by Engels from Marx's various writings and letters.

Most people will know of those two major works on

Communism, even if they never read them. By themselves, those two works constitute a treatise against capitalism and free-market societies, as well as a call to arms against the ruling and middle-classes, the so-called *bourgeoisie*, as opposed to the working classes, the *proletariat*. In those two works, Marx and Engels rather *calmly* advocated institution of their described Communist system. Little detail was provided, however, as to exactly *how* large populations could be persuaded to voluntarily give up their land, houses, savings and other property, nor to have their lives uprooted according to Marxist collectivist schemes. The *Communist Manifesto* contained a few sections which suggested how this magical transformation into a worker's paradise might be accomplished, but without too much detail.

For example, to merely state Communism would require the "abolition of private property", and "collective ownership of the means of production" gives no hint about the deployment of armed squads of Communist thugs, the "Red Army", who would beat or shoot dead anyone who dared to resist their drunken pillaging, and theft into Communist Party hands of entire villages, cities and districts. In nations where most all of the land and resources were owned by the Church or Tsar, or hereditary Lords descended from ancient conquering invaders, ideas about "redistribution" of land quite rationally grabbed the interest of ordinary farmers. Marxists promised to distribute the old feudal land holdings to them, the people who worked the land, with their hands and backs. Only after the revolutionary battles were won, however, did the peasants learn that "The State" – another vague landlord – would be the sole beneficiary of the "redistribution." *State ownership of private land and production* was to define every form of Communism, with peasant farmers being "redistributed" like cattle, to collectivist prison-farms.

Factory workers in the cities were also given great promises, but suffered a similar collectivist fate. Industrial workers in regions where unions had been suppressed warmed to the idea of Communist "worker's councils", and nearly everyone else took to the idea of "democratic Soviets", i.e., village-level self-governing councils with elected representation. Only later did they discover that the "councils" and "Soviets" would be dominated by Communist Party bosses who dictated how the shops and factories, and indeed the very lives of the working proletariat would be run, even more ruthlessly, and at lower pay than what the original capitalist bosses had paid. Whatever "democratic councils and Soviets" that sprang up spontaneously would be quickly demolished by the new Communist State. Real democracy was replaced with "democratic centralism", where elite Party bosses voted to determine how everyone else would be ruled and commanded.

None of this should have come as any surprise to those who had actually read the writings of Marx and Engels in some depth. While *Communist Manifesto* and *Das Kapital* did not openly state that mass murder, terrorism and repression would be necessary to implement Communism, their lesser-known but publicly-available publications most surely did express these exact sentiments. In those lesser-known writings, Marx and Engels unmasked, and explicitly advocated the necessity for a gargantuan slaughter, to make Communism "work". They spoke about the "racial trash" who would have to be "exterminated", of entire peoples who would be swept up in a glorious "world war-storm" or "revolutionary terror" that would bring about the Holy Crusade of Communist Paradise. Consequently, we cannot be surprised at how such totalitarian Marxian-Engelsian genocide, assassinations, Gulags and slavery later appeared within the dictatorships of Lenin, Trotsky, Stalin, Mao Zedong, Ho Chi Minh, Pol Pot, the North Korean Kims, Castro, and other despots of Communism.

In this work, I provide a selection of pertinent quotations, taken from both German originals and "Marxist-approved" English translations by others, with citations and weblinks (in the Reference section) for those who wish to confirm what is presented here. Most of these quotes are found on internet, though frequently slightly mistranslated. Consequently, I have traced each provided quote back to the most scholarly original sources I could find, double-checking everything as much as humanly possible, given how I cannot speak Russian. My wife, a native Berliner who speaks fluent German and English, double checked and in many cases corrected older translations from German. Internet in particular is filled with unattributed quotations by Marx, Engels, Lenin and Trotsky, but nothing was included here unless I could find clearly documented sources – the Genocide Quotes are, in any case, either buried within or censored from Marxist and Communist-friendly websites and publications.

Prior to composing these materials in book form, I initially submitted my findings to an internet group of scholars where I knew several dedicated Marxists were present. *My, how the sparks did fly*, as these materials, I observed, hit their world view of a "benign Communism" or "peaceful Marxism" like a hammer on thin pottery. Their objections nevertheless fell into several interesting patterns, easily refuted, but worthwhile to repeat here.

Objection 1. The quotes are cherry-picked. Certainly the quotes are selected out from their publications for the sole reason of their alarming nature. But there was no redeeming context for any of them. Also, there are no other publications by these "founding tyrants" which stand as a corrective, and which are being ignored. Did these men issue retractions or corrections? No, never, not once so far as I can determine. If a man curses "money Jews" and "niggers", and rages that whole ethnic groups and peoples he doesn't like should be exterminated, and does so in not just private letters but in published articles which get widely circulated among his followers – but he never once says in remorse "Oh My God what a stupid thing I said", or "I was drunk or feeling awful and must retract that" – then why should we ignore those statements as if they were uncharacteristic of their true and honest beliefs? And there aren't just a few of such genocidal quotes, but *dozens* of them. Many were excluded due to their repetitive nature. The quotes are not "cherry-picked" at all, and mean exactly what they say.

Objection 2. They are mistranslated. No, the quotes are accurate, often with several different translations available, all yielding the same/similar sentiments. It is up to the defenders and apologists of the "founding tyrants" to clarify exactly where a problem might exist in translation. Additionally, these quoted materials are often found on pro-Marx and pro-Communism websites, such as the big *Marxist.org* website, where they are presented uncensored – though sometimes, as I point out, with a toning-down of the most extremely harsh and vile-vicious phrases. The Marxists and Communists of today don't have any real problem with those sentiments, and openly reference them, in the same manner the neo-Nazi websites quote from Goebbels and Hitler in celebration of their views and actions – at least when not denying them.

Objection 3. They are isolated examples without meaning to larger Marxist theory. The example is given, if some famous artists were Jew-haters and black-racists, muttering ethnic hatreds to commit genocide, this would not undervalue their art. Or if a genius engineer of incredible inventions held seriously racist sentiments, this would not negate the value of their inventions. This line of argument certainly has merit. But *Marx and Engels were not inventors of devices or artwork irrelevant to their social theories and plans for the future.* Their life's work was the fomentation of violent revolutionary movements and new collectivist social institutions, and laws for oppression. In detailed arguments and theory, they laid out how this or that group was to be treated, suppressed, or eliminated. Marx, Engels, Lenin and Trotsky all wrote books and articles for their thuggish followers outlining the necessity for "revolutionary terror", and worked within political structures or secret organizations, towards obtaining guns and bombs by which their followers would kill many innocent people. They anticipated that certain ethnic groups or populations would resist Communist collectivism, and so understood the "necessity" for mass-murder to implement their cherished Communist utopia. It was taken for granted, as shown unambiguously in the quotes to follow, their utopian goals and aspirations could *only be achieved by great violence.* And indeed, history shows *great violence was used in every single case where Marxist Communism was implemented.*

Consequently, the statements of Marx and Engels openly advocating murderous violence as a "justified means to the ends", and the later words of Lenin and Trotsky written while in process of carrying out such murderous violence, are extremely important to fathom their motivations and agendas, if not also their psychopathic amorality. There is no reason to shy away from taking them at their word.

There are other matters of great significance to the Genocide Quotes. Modern Marxists and Communists frequently try to soften and white-wash the evil words and crimes of Marx, Engels, Lenin and Trotsky, *alongside a similar falsification of the terrible crimes of Stalin and Mao. And from there, to also erase the crimes of the more recent Communist dictators such as Ho Chi Minh, Pol Pot, the North Korean Kims, and Castro.* Marxists also apply false moral equivalence and falsified history, claiming Western democracy with its human rights, freedoms and free-market capitalism is "just as bad", or "no different" from the semi- or fully-feudal systems run by the old Kaisers, Emperors, Tsars and Caliphs, and by their various religious institutions in the pre-Marxist periods. Those old feudal Empires retained most land and wealth in the hands of the Kings, Churches, and their minions, something not observed within the American or French democratic Republics, where the Power of Kings and Absolutism of Church had been opposed and restrained decades earlier. In those reformed systems of free-market capitalism, the majorities of ordinary citizens could choose their own life-path, own land, retain the value of their labor, and also enjoy freedom of speech, press, voting rights and similar going back to the 1700s. The Marxist-Leninists were even more strongly against those liberal democratic Republics than they were against the remaining Kingly Empires, however, but they made good propaganda pretending they were all for freedom and democracy. In the end, all the different Marxist movements unmasked as purely Red Fascist, betraying millions into Communist slavery.

A full discussion of the various Left-faction efforts in these directions, to denigrate democracy, freedom and human rights while simultaneously promoting dictatorship, slavery and blind obedience to a godly "State", is beyond the focus of this work. But it is important to keep in mind the exceptionally greater freedoms people already enjoyed in the world's democracies at the time when Marx and Engels were laying their plans.

The reader will also observe, the various Genocide Quotes from Communist leaders of the 1800s and early 1900s are frequently indistinguishable from similar statements by other murdering tyrants of later years, such as Adolf Hitler, who rose to power in 1933. The malignant theology of Marxist Communism *began three generations before Hitlerism, however, with Marx and Engels, and was firstly applied socially by their followers Lenin and Trotsky. Only a few years later* was an even greater slaughter of innocents undertaken by Stalin, Mao, and all the other horrid Saints of Communism. *The Genocide Quotes therefore reveal the* <u>*structural nature*</u> *of murderous violence, and the chronic obliteration of individual rights and freedoms, precisely within the core of Marxist theory and thought,* even if dedicated Marxists try to cover up these facts, or chronically deny them.

Another counter-argument has been raised, that "Communism was necessary" along with its massive death-tolls, to depose the Kings and Tsars of the 19th-Century feudal Empires. Certainly those Empires had their own history of bloodshed and repression to atone for, but that line of argument rationalizing retributional mass-killings by Marxists also fails, beyond its raw immorality.

Firstly, the period of the two World Wars of the 20th Century saw the end of Empires across the Old World. The German and Austro-Hungarian Empires collapsed. The Tsar of Russia was, initially, peacefully deposed. The Ottoman Empire was broken apart. Imperial China ended as did Imperial Japan. *Those nations who followed a post-Imperial path into Communism experienced decades of additional internal massacres and bloodshed, with tens of millions of additional victims, beyond war deaths.* Nothing approaching this was experienced in the nations that moved towards democratic Republics with free market capitalism.

Secondly, even before these events, the old autocratic Kings and Tsars rarely collapsed into the intensity of barbarism seen within the Communist nations that replaced them. The Romanov Tsars were absolutely tame and tolerant by the standards of Lenin and Trotsky, who started mass-killings of oppositionists the day they shot their way into power. Mao Zedong was exceedingly more bloody and merciless against his own Chinese people than the moderate nationalist Chaing Kai-Shek. Ho Chi Minh feigned "Jeffersonian democracy" and "nationalism", but assassinated all of the authentic Vietnamese democrats and nationalists he could grasp. He ordered repeated bloody massacres of his own Vietnamese people, making the French and Americans look tame by comparison. Castro and Che were far more ruthless and murdering than Batista or other brutes of rightist Latin politics. And so on.

Thirdly, Marxists never reference the earlier successful American Revolution against the power of Kings, which after liberation did not degenerate into a nightmare of bloodlust vengeance. Even the French, whose Revolution briefly degenerated into collectivist tyranny and abuse of the guillotine, after a time got back on track towards an authentic democratic Republic, and the killings ended. *The American and French democratic revolutions owed nothing to Marx.* So too did the English embrace democracy and disempower their Queens and Kings into figureheads, and thereby avoid the butchery so prevalent following Socialist-Communist coups.

The well-being and material prosperity of people has always thrived upon democracy, individual rights and freedoms, with economic models of free-market capitalism, fine-tuned by trade unions and other reformist institutions, plus legal measures against economic corporate gangsterism and crony-piracy. Such economic crimes have been a dominating feature of every Communist nation – as with the Chinese Red Army generals acting like Mafia bosses, extorting local workers and factories under their control. The Communist Parties of the world are led by a Billionaire criminal class, something also seen in the violent Islamic world, which has yet to experience even the most modest of social reforms. They are both demonstrably far worse than the old feudal Kings and Emperors.

And therein lies a lesson from history: The human condition was never advanced by swapping the autocracy of Kingly despots with a new self-appointed supremacist power group who refused democratic and individual liberty constraints on their power, or who dispensed "justice" by collectivist mob-rule with firing squads, mass-graves, guillotines and slavery. Such has unfortunately been the grim fate, or trend, of every nation that followed the Socialist-Communist siren-song of Marx and Engels.

Another historical truth emerges along this line of analysis. There is a same-similar situation in the Islamic world today, which over nearly 1400 years of its totalitarian theocratic history has not tolerated any significant self-reform. This is so, even as self-blinded Westerners of Marxist-Communist inclinations fall all over themselves to serve up endless excuses for bloody Islamic supremacist preachings, social violence and terrorism. In this, there is a characterological attraction between those who serve International Socialism and International Islam, if not also the very similar sentiments of National Socialism.

I have kept this book short, avoiding to provide similar genocide-quotes from Stalin, Mao, the North Korean Kims, Ho Chi Minh, Castro and Che. That could easily be done, however, and might later justify a second volume.

It is my hope that these quotes from Communism's Founding Tyrants will be so shocking to the average liberal and merely misinformed Marxist, so as to horrify them, to realize what a deadly brew they have swallowed. I invite them to dig deep into the facts of Communism's bloody history, and to stop supporting social movements which, once they take root, invariably lead to rivers of blood.

James DeMeo, PhD
Greensprings, Oregon
April 2016

Civilian Death Toll from Communism in the 20th Century[§]

Soviet Union:	20 million
Peoples Republic of China	65 million
East Europe Soviet Satellites	1 million
North Korea	2 million
Vietnam (Communist)	1 million
Cambodia	2 million
Ethiopia and other Africa	1.7 million
Afghanistan	1.5 million
Cuba and Latin America	150,000
Communist movements and Parties not in power	10,000

TOTAL: **94,360,000 victims**

The estimates include executions by various means such as firing squads, hanging, drowning, battering, gassing, poisoning; destruction of populations by starvation, man-made famine, deliberate food restrictions; by forced transportation or deportation with consequent confinement and deprivation; and by forced labor in prison camps with exhaustion, illness, starvation and disease. This total does not include the deaths of combatants during wars that brought Communist regimes to power. [§]

_____

[§] Courtois, S., et al.: *The Black Book of Communism: Crimes, Terror, Repression*, Harvard U. Press, 1999, p.4.

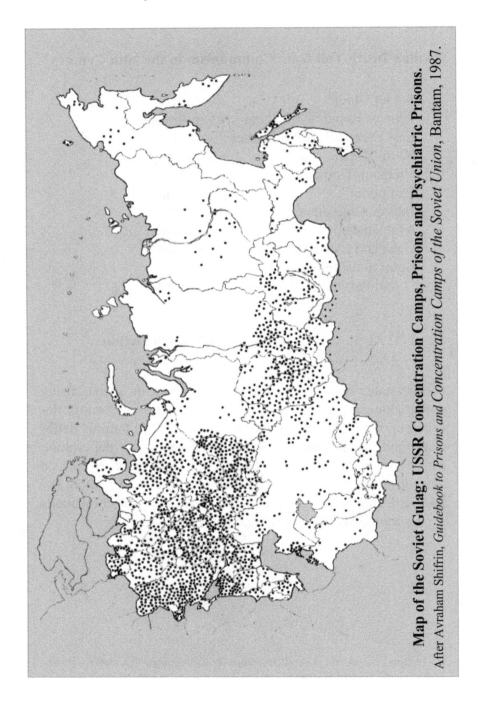

Map of the Soviet Gulag: USSR Concentration Camps, Prisons and Psychiatric Prisons.
After Avraham Shifrin, *Guidebook to Prisons and Concentration Camps of the Soviet Union*, Bantam, 1987.

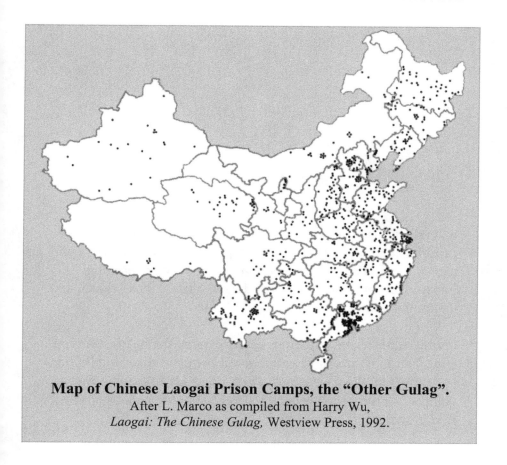

Map of Chinese Laogai Prison Camps, the "Other Gulag".
After L. Marco as compiled from Harry Wu,
Laogai: The Chinese Gulag, Westview Press, 1992.

"Our [Chinese Communist Party] economic theory holds the human being is the most fundamental productive force. Except for those who must be exterminated physically out of political consideration, human beings must be utilized as productive forces, with submissiveness as the prerequisite. The Laogai system's fundamental policy is 'Forced Labor as a means, while Thought Reform is our basic aim.'"
– Mao Zedong. Quoted in Harry Wu, "The Other Gulag", *National Review*, 4/5/1999, Vol.51, No.6, p.24-25.

So|cial|ism: 1) a political and economic theory of social organization that advocates the means of production, distribution, and exchange should be owned or regulated by the government. 2) a transitional social state between the overthrow of capitalism and the realization of communism.

Com|mu|nism: a doctrine based on revolutionary Marxian socialism and Marxism-Leninism where a centralized totalitarian state ruled by the Communist Party owns all land and property, controls the means of production, and dictates to individuals their role in society.

Quotations from Comrades Marx and Engels:

Advocating War, Slavery, Racism, Ethnic Hatred and Genocide. Mocking Justice, Freedom, Democracy and Equality. Contempt for the Poor, Workers, Farmers and Moderates.

1840-1849

"This is our calling, that we shall become the Templars of this Grail, gird the sword round our loins for its sake and stake our lives joyfully in the last, holy war which will be followed by the thousand-year reign of freedom."
   – Friedrich Engels (under pseud. F. Oswald), *Schelling and Revelation: Critique of the Latest Attempt of Reaction Against the Free Philosophy*, Ch.5 "Conclusion", Leipzig 1841.

"I am of the opinion, perhaps in contrast to many whose standpoint I share in other respects, that the reconquest of the German-speaking left bank of the Rhine is a matter of national honour, and that the Germanisation of a disloyal Holland and of Belgium is a political necessity for us. Shall we let the German nationality be completely suppressed in these countries, while the Slavs are rising ever more powerfully in the East?"
   – Friedrich Engels (under pseud. F. Oswald), "Telegraph für Deutschland" No.5, Jan. 1841.

Karl Marx

"Democracy is, as I take all forms of government to be, a contradiction in itself, an untruth, nothing but hypocrisy (theology, as we Germans call it), at the bottom. Political liberty is sham-liberty, the worst possible sort of slavery; the appearance of liberty, and therefore the worst servitude. Just so also is political equality for me; therefore democracy, as well as every other form of government, must ultimately break to pieces... we must have either a regular slavery – that is, an undisguised despotism, or real liberty, and real equality – that is, Communism. ...it did not succeed, because... the public mind was not yet far enough advanced."

– Friedrich Engels, "I. France", *The New Moral World: Progress of Social Reform On the Continent,* No.19, 4 November 1843.

"Let us consider the actual, worldly Jew – not the Sabbath Jew, as Bauer does, but the everyday Jew. ... What is the worldly religion of the Jew? Huckstering. What is his worldly God? Money..... Money is the jealous god of Israel, in face of which no other god may exist. Money degrades all the gods of man – and turns them into commodities.... The bill of exchange is the real god of the Jew. His god is only an illusory bill of exchange.... The chimerical nationality of the Jew is the nationality of the merchant, of the man of money in general."

– Karl Marx, "On the Jewish Question", *Deutsch-Französische Jahrbücher*; 1844.

Friedrich Engels

"Firstly, the farmers, the most stupid set of people in existence, who, clinging to feudal prejudices, burst forth in masses, ready to die rather than cease to obey those whom they, their fathers and grandfathers, had called their masters; and submitted to be trampled on and horse-whipped by."
– Friedrich Engels, Letter to

Editor: "The State of Germany", *The Northern Star*. No.415, 25 Oct.1845.

"The proletarians, driven to despair, will seize the torch which Stephens has preached to them; the vengeance of the people will come down with a wrath of which the rage of 1795 gives no true idea. The war of the poor against the rich will be the bloodiest ever waged."
  – Friedrich Engels, "The Attitude of the Bourgeoisie Towards the Proletariat", *Condition of the Working Class in England*, 1845.

"As for slavery, there is no need for me to speak of its bad aspects. The only thing requiring explanation is the good side of slavery. I do not mean indirect slavery, the slavery of proletariat; I mean direct slavery, the slavery of the Blacks in Surinam, in Brazil, in the southern regions of North America. Direct slavery is as much the pivot upon which our present-day industrialism turns as are machinery, credit, etc. ... Slavery is therefore an economic category of paramount importance."
  – Karl Marx, Letter to Pavel Vasilyevich Annenkov, 28 December 1846.

"...there is only one way in which the murderous death agonies of the old society and the bloody birth throes of the new society can be shortened, simplified and concentrated, and that way is revolutionary terrorism."
  – Karl Marx, "The Victory of the Counter-Revolution in Vienna," *Neue Rheinische Zeitung*, No.136, 7 November 1848.

"The Communists disdain to conceal their views and aims. They openly declare that their ends can be attained only by the forcible overthrow of all existing social conditions."

– Karl Marx & Friedrich Engels, in *Communist Manifesto,* Chapter 4: "Position of the Communists in Relation to the Various Existing Opposition Parties", 1848.

"By the same right under which France took Flanders, Lorraine and Alsace, and will sooner or later take Belgium – by that same right Germany takes over Schleswig; it is the right of civilization as against barbarism, of progress as against stability. Even if the agreements were in Denmark's favor – which is very doubtful – this right carries more weight than all the agreements, for it is the right of historical evolution."

– Friedrich Engels, "The Danish-Prussian Armistice", *Neue Rheinische Zeitung,* 10. Sep. 1848.

"And as for the Jews, who since the emancipation of their sect have everywhere put themselves, at least in the person of their eminent representatives, at the head of the counter-revolution – what awaits them? There has been no waiting for victory in order to throw them back into their ghetto. In Bromberg the Government is renewing the old restrictions on freedom of movement and thus robbing the Jews of one of the first of Rights of Man of 1789, the right to move freely from one place to another."

– Karl Marx , "Confessions of a Noble Soul", *Neue Rheinische Zeitung,* No.145, 17 Nov. 1848.

"Every provisional political set-up following a revolution requires a dictatorship, and an energetic dictatorship at that."

– Karl Marx, *Neue Rheinische Zeitung* 14 Sep. 1848.

"Among all the nations and sub-nations of Austria, only three standard-bearers of progress took an active part in history, and are still capable of life – the Germans, the Poles and the

Magyars. **Hence they are now revolutionary. All the other large and small nationalities and peoples are destined to perish before long in the world revolutionary war-storm. For that reason they are now counter-revolutionary. ... these** *racial trash* **always become fanatical standard-bearers of counter-revolution and remain so until their complete extirpation or loss of national identity, just as their whole existence in general is itself a protest against a great historical revolution. ... The next world war will result in the disappearance from the face of the earth not only of reactionary classes and dynasties, but also of entire reactionary peoples. And that, too, is a step forward."**

– Friedrich Engels, "The Magyar Struggle," *Neue Rheinische Zeitung*, 13 Jan. 1849.

[Author's Note:

1. On the above quote, the "racial trash" whom Engels (and Marx, who edited the *NRZ* journal and approved its publication) wanted to "perish" and "disappear" were mentioned in the article, and included the Scottish Highlanders, Bretons, Basques, South Slavs, Slovenes, Croats, Serbs and Czechs.

2. Some of the more extreme language and terms used by Engels in this article have been frequently mistranslated by Marxist apologists in a greatly softened manner, erasing the full viciousness of their meanings. For example the phrase "im revolutionären Weltsturm unterzugehen" is generally translated as "to perish in a revolutionary world storm". But these English words don't truly capture the intensity of the original German. "Weltsturm" carries the meaning of a major widespread war-catastrophe with massive deaths, reinforced by the term "unterzugehen" in the original German, which in this context means "to perish". It is therefore translated here as "world revolutionary war-storm". Likewise, the term *"Völkerabfälle"* given italicized emphasis in Engels' original text, carries the meaning of "human trash" or "garbage people", and is quite a severe term indicating he viewed such people as "scum" or "subhuman", destined to "disappear from the face of the earth"

once the forthcoming Marxist revolutionary *weltsturm* took place. Marxists often mistranslate "Völkerabfälle" into softer or confused English, such as "petty hidebound nations" or "residual fragments of peoples". This can only be viewed as an effort to conceal the truly vicious and hate-filled sentiments of Engels and Marx. The context is quite clear what they intended – *genocide* – reinforced by the other quotations given herein.

3. This article and quote is often wrongly attributed to Marx, perhaps because Engels' article was firstly printed in the German journal edited by Marx, the *Neue Rheinische Zeitung*.]

Neue Rheinische Zeitung.
Organ der Demokratie.

"Germans and Magyars [of the Austro-Hungarian Empire] united all these small, stunted and impotent little nations into a single big state and thereby enabled them to take part in a historical development from which, left to themselves, they would have remained completely aloof! Of course, matters of this kind cannot be accomplished without many a tender national blossom being forcibly broken. But in history nothing is achieved without violence and implacable ruthlessness... In short, it turns out these "crimes" of the Germans and Magyars against the said Slavs are among the best and most praiseworthy deeds which our [German] and the Magyar people can boast in their history. ... To the sentimental phrases about brotherhood which we are being offered here on behalf of the most counter-revolutionary nations of Europe, we reply that hatred of Russians was and still is the primary revolutionary passion among Germans; that since the revolution hatred of Czechs and Croats has been added, and that only by the most determined use of terror against these Slav peoples can we, jointly with the Poles and Magyars, safeguard the revolution. ... Then there will be a struggle, an "unrelenting life-and-death struggle" against those Slavs who betray the revolution; an annihilating fight and most determined terrorism — not in the interests of Germany, but in the interests of the revolution!"

– Friedrich Engels, "Democratic Pan-Slavism," *Neue Rheinische Zeitung*, No.222, 14. Feb. 1849.

"We discovered that in connection with these figures the German national simpletons and money-grubbers of the Frankfurt parliamentary swamp always counted as Germans the Polish Jews as well, although this dirtiest of all races, neither by its jargon nor by its descent, but at most only through its lust for profit, could have any relation of kinship with Frankfurt."

– Friedrich Engels, *Neue Rheinische Zeitung*, 29 April 1849.

"We have no compassion and we ask no compassion from you. When our turn comes, we shall not make excuses for the terror."

– Karl Marx & Friedrich Engels "Suppression of the *Neue Rheinische Zeitung*," *Neue Rheinische Zeitung*, 19 May 1849.

1850-1859

"[The working class] must act in such a manner that the revolutionary excitement does not collapse immediately after the victory. On the contrary, they must maintain it as long as possible. Far from opposing so-called excesses, such as sacrificing to popular revenge of hated individuals or public buildings to which hateful memories are attached, such deeds must not only be tolerated, but their direction must be taken in hand, for examples' sake."

– Karl Marx, *Address to the Communist League*, 1850. Cited in E. Burns (Ed.), *A Handbook of Marxism*, 1935, p.66, 135ff.

"From the first moment of victory, we must no longer direct our distrust against the beaten reactionary enemy, but against our former allies (i.e., democratic Socialists). ...The arming of the whole proletariat with rifles, guns, and ammunition should be carried out at once ... the workers must ... organize themselves into an independent guard, with their own chiefs and general staff. ...that the bourgeois democratic Government not only immediately loses all backing among the workers, but from the commencement finds itself under the supervision and threats of authorities behind whom stands the entire mass of the working class. ...As soon as the new Government is established they will commence to fight the workers. In order that this party (i.e., the democrats) whose betrayal of the workers will begin with the first hour of victory, should be frustrated in its nefarious work, it is necessary to organize and arm the proletariat."

– Karl Marx, *Address to the Communist League*, 1850. Cited in E. Burns (Ed.), *A Handbook of Marxism*, 1935, p.67.

"It would perhaps be as well if things were to remain quiet for a few years yet, so that all this 1848 democracy has time to rot away."

– Karl Marx letter to Joseph Weydemayer, 27 June 1851.

"May the devil take these peoples' movements, especially when they are 'peaceful'"

– Karl Marx letter to Friedrich Engels, 4 Feb. 1852.

"There are no bigger donkeys than these workers.... Look at our 'craftsmen'; Sad that world history should be be made with such people."

– Karl Marx letter to Adolf Cluss, 20.Jul.1852.

"Society is undergoing a silent revolution, which must be submitted to, and which takes no more notice of the human existences it breaks down than an earthquake regards the

houses it subverts. The classes and the races, too weak to master the new conditions of life, must give way."
– Karl Marx, "Forced Emigration", *New York Daily Tribune,* 22 March 1853.

"Even with Europe in decay, still a war should have roused the healthy elements; a war should have awakened a lot of hidden powers, and surely so much energy would have been present among 250 million people that at least a respectable battle would have occurred, in which both parties could have reaped some honor, as much honor as courage and bravery can gain on the battlefield."
– Karl Marx & Friedrich Engels, "The Boring War", *New York Daily Tribune,* 17 Aug.1854.

"Thus we find every tyrant backed by a Jew, as is every pope by a Jesuit. In truth, the cravings of oppressors would be hopeless, and the practicability of war out of the question, if there were not an army of Jesuits to smother thought and a handful of Jews to ransack pockets. The fact that 1855 years ago Christ drove the Jewish moneychangers out of the temple, and that the moneychangers of our age enlisted on the side of tyranny happen again chiefly to be Jews, is perhaps no more than a historical coincidence. The loan-mongering Jews of Europe do only on a larger and more obnoxious scale what many others do on one smaller and less significant. But it is only because the Jews are so strong that it is timely and expedient to expose and stigmatize their organization."

23

– Karl Marx, "The Russian Loan", *New York Daily Tribune,* 4 January 1856. [Author's Note: So embarrassing is this article to Marxists that they have scrubbed it from all public archives.]

"Those dogs of democrats and liberal riff-raff will see that we're the only chaps who haven't been stultified by the ghastly period of peace."
– Karl Marx letter to Friedrich Engels, 25 February 1859.

1860-1869

"This young lady, who instantly overwhelmed me with her kindness, is the ugliest creature I have seen in my entire life, with repulsive Jewish facial features."
– Karl Marx letter to Antoinette Philips, 24 March 1861.

"...the Jewish Nigger, Lassalle... it is now completely clear to me that he, as is proved by his cranial formation and his hair, descends from the Negroes from Egypt, assuming that his mother or grandmother had not interbred with a nigger. Now this union of Judaism and Germanism with a basic Negro substance must produce a peculiar product. The obtrusiveness of the fellow is also nigger-like."
– Karl Marx letter to Friedrich Engels, 30 July 1862, in reference to his socialist political competitor, Ferdinand Lassalle.

"...without doubt [Colonel Lapinski] is the cleverest Pole – besides being an homme d'action – that I have ever met. His sympathies are all on the German side, though in manners and speech he is also a Frenchman. He cares nothing for the struggle of nationalities and only knows the racial struggle. He hates all Orientals, among whom he numbers Russians Turks, Greeks, Armenians, etc., with equal impartiality.... His aim now is to raise a German legion in London..."
– Karl Marx letter to Friedrich Engels, 12 September 1863.

"Our fatherland looks damned pitiful. Without a thrashing [war] from outside nothing can be achieved with these sons-of-bitches."
– Karl Marx to Friedrich Engels, 12 September 1863.

"Russia is a name usurped by the Muscovites. They are not Slavs; they do not belong to the Indo-Germanic race at all, they are des intrus [intruders], who must be chased back across the Dnieper, etc."
– Karl Marx letter to Friedrich Engels, 24 June 1865.

"One could laugh oneself sick about his stories of the nigger Santa Maria and of the transmutations of the whites into Negroes. Especially, that the traditions of the Senegal niggers deserve absolute credulity, just because the rascals cannot write! . . . Perhaps this man will prove in the second volume, how he explains the fact, that we Rhinelanders have not long ago turned into idiots and niggers on our own Devonian Transition rocks . . . Or perhaps he will maintain that we are real niggers."
– Friedrich Engels letter to Karl Marx, 2 October 1866.

"I will chew out Wilhelm [Liebknecht] with a few lines about his feebleness. For what we want is exactly the demise of the 'Social-Democrat' and of all that Lassalle-crap."
– Karl Marx letter to Friedrich Engels, 10 February 1866.

1870-1879

"The Lumpenproletariat [rag-proletariat, violent criminal-class low income people], this residue of the degenerated members of all classes that has its headquarters in the big cities, is the worst of all possible allies. This riff-raff is totally for sale and totally obnoxious."
– Karl Marx: "General Council to the Federal Council of Romance Switzerland", 1 Jan.1870.

"The French need a thrashing. If the Prussians win, the centralisation of the state power will be useful for the centralisation of the German working class. German predominance would also transfer the centre of gravity of the workers' movement in Western Europe from France to Germany, and one has only to compare the movement in the two countries from 1866 till now to see that the German working class is superior to the French both theoretically and organisationally. Their [German] predominance over the French on the world stage would also mean the predominance of our theory over Proudhon's, etc."

– Karl Marx letter to Friedrich Engels, 20 July 1870.

"Have these gentlemen ever seen a revolution? A revolution is certainly the most authoritarian thing there is; it is an act whereby one part of the population imposes its will upon the other part by means of rifles, bayonets and cannon, all of which are highly authoritarian means. And the victorious party must maintain its rule by means of the terror which its arms inspire in the reactionaries. Would the Paris Commune have lasted more than a day if it had not used the authority of the armed people against the bourgeoisie? Cannot we, on the contrary, blame it for having made too little use of that authority?"

– Friedrich Engels: Quoted by V. Lenin, *The State and Revolution, Supplementary Explanations by Engels,* 2. "Controversy with the Anarchists", 1873.

"The man is too wise. And on top of that, such offensive, vulgar, democratic arguments! To denigrate violence as something to be rejected, when we all know that in the end nothing can be achieved without violence!"

– Friedrich Engels letter to Wilhelm Blos, 21 February 1874.

"That a host of somewhat muddled and purely democratic demands should figure in the programme, some of them being

**Executions of Catholic Clergy by
Comrades of the Paris Commune, March-May 1871.**

The Paris Commune developed in the wake of social chaos following France's defeat during the Franco-Prussian War, and collapse of Napoleon III's Second Empire. Paris had been under siege by the Prussian army, and a National Guard had been formed from its citizens. Post-war elections in March led to a victory of revolutionary elements who formed a communard government, declaring itself independent from the French government of Versailles. Many social reforms were enacted, alongside decidedly Marxist confiscatory and other collectivist policies. Similar communes appeared in Lyon, Marseilles, Toulouse and elsewhere, but only the Paris Commune dared to oppose the reformed Versailles government, erecting barricades and forming an armed resistance.

French government troops soon attacked and re-took the city in a week of bloody fighting, during which time each side committed atrocities against captured soldiers. The Communards also took mob vengeance against loyalist government, military, police and church leaders, burning homes and government buildings.

Marx and Engels became ecstatic over the news of the Paris uprising, their own writings and rhetoric rationalizing and praising the bloody revolution and murder. In later decades, Lenin and Trotsky would also write glowingly about the bloodshed of the Paris Commune, to help rationalize their own mass-murder and genocides.

of a purely fashionable nature — for instance 'legislation by the people' such as exists in Switzerland and does more harm than good, if it can be said to do anything at all.... Now, since the state is merely a transitional institution of which use is made in the struggle, in the revolution, to keep down one's enemies by force, it is utter madness to speak of a free people's state; so long as the proletariat still makes use of the state, it makes use of it, not for the purpose of freedom, but of keeping down its enemies."

– Friedrich Engels letter to August Bebel, 18-28 March 1875.

"For when the little chap (Wedde) was in London for the first time I used the expression 'modern mythology' to describe the goddesses of 'Justice, Freedom, Equality, etc.' who were now all the rage again; this made a deep impression on him, as he has himself done much in the service of these higher beings."

– Karl Marx letter to Friedrich Engels, 1 August 1877.

"The compromise with the followers of Lassalle has also led to compromises with other half-baked elements, ...but also with a whole gang of immature students and overly wise PhDs who want to give a 'higher, ideal' twist to socialism, i.e. to replace its materialistic foundation through modern mythology with their goddesses of Justice, Liberty, Equality and fraternité [brotherhood] .... The workers themselves, when they give up working and become professional literati like Mr. Most and his ilk, always incite 'theoretical' trouble and are always ready to attach themselves to muddleheads from the alleged 'learned' caste."

– Karl Marx letter to Friedrich Adolph Sorge, 19 October 1877.

"Well, then, to carry out the principles of socialism do its believers advocate assassination and bloodshed? 'No great movement,' Karl answered, 'has ever been inaugurated Without Bloodshed.'"

– Interview with Karl Marx, *Chicago Tribune*, 5 January 1879.

1880-1889

"Don't forget any affront done to you and to all our people, the time of revenge will come and must be put to good use."
– Friedrich Engels letter to August Bebel, 25 August 1881.

"The redeeming feature of war is that it puts a nation to the test. As exposure to the atmosphere reduces all mummies to instant dissolution, so war passes supreme judgment upon social systems that have outlived their vitality."
– Karl Marx, "The Eastern Question", 24 Sept 1885.

"The capitalist knows that all commodities, however shabby they may look, or however badly they may smell, are, in belief and in truth, money – inwardly circumcised Jews – and also a miraculous means to make more money out of money."
– Karl Marx, published posthumously, *Das Kapital,,* Volume One, Part II: The Transformation of Money and Capital, Ch.4: The General Formula for Capital, 1867. [Author's Note: Marx frequently inserted hateful and derogatory references to Jews when speaking about commodities or money.]

"Being in his quality as a nigger, a degree nearer to the rest of the animal kingdom than the rest of us, he is undoubtedly the most appropriate representative of that district."
– Friedrich Engels letter to Karl Marx's daughter, Laura, speaking about her husband Paul Lafargue, April 1887. [Author's Note: Lafargue ran for public office in the district encompassing the Paris Zoo. Engels felt license to write such filth to Laura (Marx) Lafargue, because Karl Marx himself had so violently opposed her marriage to "a nigger". Marx also referenced Lafargue as "the little negro" or "the gorilla". Jenny Marx, the mother, wrote to Engels that she hoped her daughter would not have "ten little nigger boys". Apparently this kind of serious racism ran deep in the Marx family, except for Laura Marx.]

"No war is any longer possible for Prussia-Germany except a world war and a world war indeed of an extent and violence hitherto undreamt of. Eight to ten millions of soldiers will massacre one another and in doing so devour the whole of Europe until they have stripped it barer than any swarm of locusts has ever done. The devastations of the Thirty Years' War compressed into three or four years, and spread over the whole Continent; famine, pestilence, general demoralisation both of the armies and of the mass of the people produced by acute distress; hopeless confusion of our artificial machinery in trade, industry and credit, ending in general bankruptcy; collapse of the old states and their traditional state wisdom to such an extent that crowns will roll by dozens on the pavement and there will be no body to pick them up; absolute impossibility of foreseeing how it will all end and who will come out of the struggle as victor; only one result is absolutely certain: general exhaustion and the establishment of the conditions for the ultimate victory of the working class."

– Friedrich Engels, London, 15 December 1887. Quoted by V.I. Lenin, "Prophetic Words", *Pravda*, 2 July 1918.

Quotations from Comrades Lenin & Trotsky

Putting Marx & Engels into Practice:

Instituting a Reign of Terror, Assassinations, Slavery, Mass-Murder & Genocide. Usurping Democracy. Imprisonment or Murder of Counter-Revolutionaries, Resisters, Opponents. Stealing Food from Starving Farmers. Executions of Surrendered & Wounded Soldiers, Prostitutes, Alcoholics, Peasants, Workers, Villagers & Ethnic Groups. Mass Deportations to Siberia.

1900-1919

"In an affair of this kind the last thing we need are schemes, and discussions and talk... What we need is furious energy....

I am horrified, absolutely horrified, to see people talking bombs for over six months and not a single bomb made yet."
– V.I. Lenin "Should We Organize the Revolution?", February 1905.

The young Vladimir Lenin, first to apply Marxist genocidal terrorism across Russia.

"[The revolutionary] must arm themselves as best they can (rifles, revolvers, bombs, knives, knuckle-dusters, sticks, rags soaked in kerosene for starting fires... barbed wire, nails against cavalry)... or ac-

ids to be poured on the police... The killing of spies, policemen, gendarmes, the blowing up of police stations..."

– V.I. Lenin, "Tasks of Revolutionary Army Contingents" October 1905, published firstly in *Lenin Miscellany V.*, 1922.

"We would be deceiving both ourselves and the people if we concealed from the masses the necessity of a desperate, bloody war of extermination, as the immediate task of the coming revolutionary action."

– V. I. Lenin, "Lessons of the Moscow Uprising," *Proletary*, No.2, 29 August 1906.

"[There must be] real, nation-wide terror, which reinvigorates the country."

– V.I. Lenin, 1908. Quoted in Robert Conquest, *Reflections on a Ravaged Century*, Norton, 2000, p.98.

"...in certain conditions the class struggle... [calls] for ruthless extermination of its enemies in open armed clashes."

– V.I. Lenin, "Lessons of the Commune", *Zagranichnaya Gazeta*, Geneva #2, 23 March 1908.

"To reject war in principle is un-Marxist. Who objectively stands to gain from the slogan 'Peace'? ...not the revolutionary proletariat."

– V.I. Lenin, Letter to Alexander Shliapnikov, November 1914. Quoted by Aleksandr Solzhenitsyn, *Warning to the West,* Farrar, Straus & Giroux, NY 1976, p.70.

"We cannot support the slogan 'Peace' since it is a totally muddled one and a hindrance to the revolutionary struggle."

– V.I. Lenin, letter to Alexandra Kollontai, July 1915. Quoted by Aleksandr Solzhenitsyn, *Warning to the West,* Farrar, Straus & Giroux, NY 1976, p.70.

"The aim of socialism is not only to abolish the present division of mankind into small states and all national isolation; not only to bring the nations closer to each other, but also to merge them."
– V.I. Lenin, "The Socialist Revolution and the Right of Nations to Self-Determination", *Vorbote* No. 2, April 1916.

"Our slogan must be: arming of the proletariat to defeat, expropriate and disarm the bourgeoisie. These are the only tactics possible for a revolutionary class..."
– V.I. Lenin, "The Disarmament Slogan", *Sbornik Sotsial-Demokrata* No.2, Dec.1916.

"... whoever recognizes class war must recognize civil wars, which in any class society represent the natural and, in certain circumstances, inevitable continuation, development and sharpening of class war."
– V.I. Lenin, Sept. 1916. Quoted in Dmitri Volkogonov, *Lenin: A New Biography* Free Press, 1994, p.196.

"But couldn't this correlation [of political and social forces] be altered? Say, through the subjection or extermination of some classes of society?"
– Feliks Dzerzhinsky, head of Lenin's Cheka secret police, August 1917. Quoted in George Leggett, *The Cheka: Lenin's Political Police*, Clarendon Press, 1981, p.252.

"No kind of revolutionary government could dispense with the death penalty as applied to exploiters (ie, landowners and capitalists)."
– V.I. Lenin, October 1917. Quoted in George Leggett, *The Cheka: Lenin's Political Police*, Clarendon Press, 1981, p.62.
[Author's Note: The Russian death penalty had been banished by the post-Tsarist Kerensky Provisional Government following the original February 1917 democratic Russian Revolution. Lenin objected to this, and argued shortly after the October Bolshevik

Romanticized version of Lenin's "heroic" arrival on 16 April 1917, at Finland Station in St. Petersburg (Petrograd), after years of Tsarist exile in Switzerland. In reality, Lenin arrived in the dark of night, to a small contingent of devoted followers, and subsequently plotted treason against his fellow Russians. The German High Command and Kaiser had secretly financed Lenin's return to Russia from Switzerland, in a sealed train car granted direct travel through German territory. The Germans also provided large quantities of gold to Lenin, with the assignment to launch his Bolshevik destabilization of the early Russian democracy, and pull Russian troops out of WW1. Prior to Lenin's arrival, the Romanov Tsar had been removed from power via a bloodless democratic February-March revolution, with establishment of a Russian Provisional Government, a democratic Duma parliament and democratic *Soviets* (regional and village-level councils). Lenin schemed to have the Soviets break away from and abolish the Provisional Government, after which, under his command, the Soviet councils were in turn betrayed into a bloody Bolshevik dictatorship. Lenin promised "Bread, Land, Peace." The people of Russia got little bread, and no land or peace. .

coup, that the death penalty should be reinstated and expanded. By June 1918, his power fully secured, Lenin restored the death penalty in terms far more extensive than what existed under the prior Tsars, allowing his Chekist divisions to engage in routine extrajudicial executions, "on the spot".]

"There is no point in proposing a benign program of pious wishes for peace without at the same time placing at the forefront the call for illegal organization and the summons to civil war."
 – V.I. Lenin, c.1917. Quoted by Aleksandr Solzhenitsyn, *Warning to the West,* Farrar, Straus & Giroux, NY 1976, p.70.

"You, comrade sailors, are the pride and glory of the Russian Revolution. You are its best promoters and defenders. By your deeds, by your devotion to communism, by your ruthless hatred and massacres of all exploiters and enemies of the proletariat, you have written deathless pages in the history of the Revolution. Now there is before you a new task — to sweep the Revolution free from all its enemies, to overthrow the capitalistic Government, to push the revolution to its ultimate limits, to create the kingdom of communism, the dictatorship of the proletariat and to start a world-revolution. The great drama has begun. Victory and everlasting glory call us. Let our enemies tremble. No pity, no mercy for them. Summon all your hatred. Destroy them once and forever!"
 –Leon Trotsky, 7-8 Nov.1917, a speech to soldiers gathered outside the Tsar's old Winter Palace

The Young Leon Trotsky, Lenin's executioner, later head of the ruthless Red Army.

35

in St. Petersburg: Quoted in Pitirim Sorokin, *Leaves from a Russian Diary,* Beacon Press, Boston 1950, p.62-63. [Author's Note: According to Sorokin, who was there and heard the speech, "Streets surrounding the Palace and its large courtyard were full of soldiers and sailors, and standing up in an automobile was Trotzky, haranguing the men from Kronstadt.... A wild animal roar was the answer to this speech."]

"War to the death against the rich and their hangers-on, the bourgeois intellectuals"
– V.I. Lenin, written in Dec.1917, first published as "How to Organise Competition?" *Pravda* No.17, January 20, 1929.

"Let them shoot on the spot every tenth man guilty of idleness."
– V.I. Lenin, December 1917, in a tract on the Paris Commune. Quoted in George Leggett, *The Cheka: Lenin's Political Police,* Clarendon Press, 1981, p.55.

"There is nothing immoral in the proletariat finishing off the dying class... In not more than a month's time terror will assume very violent forms, after the example of the great French Revolution; our enemies will not face prison, but the guillotine which makes man shorter by a head."
– Leon Trotsky, 1 Dec.1917. Quoted in George Leggett, *The Cheka: Lenin's Political Police,* Clarendon Press, 1981, p.54.

"Until we apply terror to speculators – shooting on the spot – we won't get anywhere."
– V.I. Lenin, 14 January 1918, in a speech to the Prisidium of the Petrograd Soviet. Quoted in George Leggett, *The Cheka: Lenin's Political Police,* Clarendon Press, 1981, p.55.

"[Take for slave-labor] able bodied bourgeoisie, men and women... [shoot] enemy agents, speculators, thugs, hooligans, counter-revolutionary agitators, German spies... Surely you

do not imagine that we shall be victorious without applying the most cruel revolutionary terror?"

– V.I. Lenin, Decree of 21 Feb. 1918. Quoted in George Leggett, *The Cheka: Lenin's Political Police*, Clarendon Press, 1981, p.56-57.

"I come to the inescapable conclusion that we must now launch the most decisive and merciless battle against the Black Hundreds clergy and crush their resistance with such ferocity that they will not forget it for several decades... The bigger the number of reactionary clergy and reactionary bourgeois we manage to shoot in the process, the better."

– V.I. Lenin, 23 Feb.1918. Quoted in Dmitri Volkogonov, *Trotsky: The Eternal Revolutionary*, Harper Collins, 1996, p.227.

"You can tell Ter [a Cheka commander] that if there is an offensive, he must make all preparations to burn Baku down totally, and this should be announced in print in Baku."

– V.I. Lenin, 3 June 1918. Quoted in Dmitri Volkogonov, *Lenin: A New Biography*, Free Press 1994, p.202.

At Lower Right: Trotsky meets with the German High Command in early March 1918, to sign the Treaty of Brest-Litovsk, making peace between the new Soviet Union and Germany. In the agreement, Germany got huge portions of industrialized and mineral-rich Western Russia, with large populations, an apparent payback for German financing of Lenin's Bolshevik coup. After Germany was defeated on the battlefield by the Allies in November of the same year, the Treaty was nullified and the lands returned to the Soviet Union.

Above, Lubyanka Prison, Moscow, in later Soviet times. Home of Lenin's Soviet secret police, the Cheka, and later Stalin's KGB. Political prisoners were dragged there, interrogated, tortured and murdered. Few who entered came out alive.

Below: A group of Chekist officer-assassins make target practice in one of the open courtyards of Lubyanka Prison.

Lenin Trotsky Quotations

Felix Dzerzhinsky, head of the Soviet *Cheka*, Lenin's murdering secret police.

"Root out the counterrevolutionaries without mercy, lock up suspicious characters in concentration camps... Shirkers will be shot, regardless of past service..."
– Leon Trotsky, 4 Aug. 1918. Order to the Commander at Vologda. Quoted in Dmitri Volkogonov, *Trotsky: The Eternal Revolutionary*, Harper Collins, 1996, p.213.

Lenin sends telegrams "to introduce mass terror" in response to civilian uprisings, and to "crush" landowners who protested requisition of their grain by military detachments. "...shoot and transport hundreds of prostitutes who got soldiers drunk, ex-officers... make mass searches... execute for possession of weapons... massively deport Mensheviks and unreliable elements. ... carry out merciless mass terror against kulaks, priests, and White Guards as well as to lock up unreliable elements in a concentration camp outside of town."
– V.I. Lenin, 9-10 August 1918, telegram to the Penza *Gubispolkom*. Quoted in Arno Meyer, *The Furies: Violence and Terror in the French and Russian Revolutions*, Princeton U. Press, 2002, p.277; and in George Leggett, *The Cheka: Lenin's Political Police*, Clarendon Press, 1981, p.103.

"Comrades! The kulak uprising in your five districts must be crushed without pity... You must make example of these people. 1) Hang (I mean hang publicly, so that people see) at least 100 kulaks, rich bastards, and known bloodsuckers. 2) Publish their names. 3) Seize all their grain. 4) Take hostages per my instructions in yesterday's telegram. Do all this so that for miles around people see it all, understand it, tremble, and tell themselves that we are killing the bloodthirsty kulaks. Telegraph your receipt and implementation.
Yours, Lenin.
P.S. Find truly hard people."
 – V.I. Lenin letter to V.V. Kuraev, Ye Bosh and A.E. Minkin, 11 August 1918. Quoted in Richard Pipes, *The Unknown Lenin: From the Secret Archive,* Yale Univ. Press, 1998, p.50.

"The Berliners will send us more money: if the scum delay, complain to me formally."
 – V.I. Lenin letter to Ya. A. Berzin, Soviet Mission in Switzerland, 14 August 1918. [Author's Note: This is the only known reference by Lenin to the German governments' secret financing of the Bolshevik movement. Lenin used the Soviet Mission in Switzerland to promote defeatist propaganda in France and the UK, serving his German financiers and masters. See Richard Pipes, *The Unknown Lenin: From the Secret Archive,* Yale Univ. Press, 1998, p.53 & 58.]

"...one out of every ten people guilty of parasitism should be executed on he spot... Merciless war against these kulaks! Death to them!"
 – V.I. Lenin, August 1918. Quoted in Dmitri Volkogonov, *Lenin: A New Biography* Free Press, 1994, p.197.

"...slaughter of those wounded fighting against you... anyone raising the sword against the existing order will perish by the sword."
 – V.I. Lenin, in *Izvestia,* 23 August 1918. Quoted in Arno

Meyer, *The Furies: Violence and Terror in the French and Russian Revolutions*, Princeton U. Press, 2002, p.277.

"...secretly and urgently to prepare the terror".
– V.I. Lenin, 3-4 September 1918, in an order to Bolshevik death-squads. Quoted in Richard Pipes, *The Unknown Lenin: From the Secret Archive,* Yale Univ. Press, 1998, p.56.

"1. Citizens who refuse to give their names are to be shot on the spot without trial; 2. The penalty of hostage-taking should be announced and they are to be shot when arms are not surrendered; 3. In the event of concealed arms being found, shoot the eldest worker in the family on the spot and without trial; 4. Any family which harboured a bandit is subject to arrest and deportation from the province, their property to be confiscated and the eldest worker in the family to be shot without trial; 5. The eldest worker of any families hiding members of the family or the property of bandits is to be shot on the spot without trial."
– V.I. Lenin, "Order for Intensified Red Terror", *Pravda*, 4 September 1918.

"I am confident that the suppression of the Kazan Czechs and White Guards, and likewise of the bloodsucking kulaks who support them, will be a model of mercilessness."
– V.I. Lenin letter to Trotsky, 8 September 1918. Quoted in George Leggett, *The Cheka: Lenin's Political Police*, Clarendon Press, 1981, p.119.

"To overcome of our enemies we must have our own socialist militarism. We must carry along with us 90 million out of the 100 million of Soviet Russia's population. As for the rest, we have nothing to say to them. They must be annihilated."
– Grigory Zinoviev, top collaborator with Lenin, September 1918. Quoted in George Leggett, *The Cheka: Lenin's Political Police* , Oxford University Press, 1986, p.114.

"Dictatorship is rule based directly on force and unrestricted by any laws. The revolutionary dictatorship of the proletariat is rule won and maintained through the use of violence by the proletariat against the bourgeoisie, rule that is unrestricted by any laws."

– V.I. Lenin. *The Proletarian Revolution and the Renegade Kautsky,* Moscow, October 1918. Quoted in Stephan Courtois, Editor "Conclusion," in *The Black Book of Communism,* Harvard University Press, 1999, p.741.

"The dictatorship of the proletariat, the proletarian state, which is a machine for the suppression of the bourgeoisie by the proletariat, is not a 'form of governing', but a state of a different type. Suppression is necessary because the bourgeoisie will always furiously resist being expropriated."

– V.I. Lenin. *The Proletarian Revolution and the Renegade Kautsky,* Moscow, October 1918.

"These Cains [Don Cossacks] must be annihilated, no mercy must be shown to any settlement that gives resistance. Mercy only for those who hand over their weapons voluntarily and come over to our side... You must cleanse the Don of the black stain of treason within a few days."

– Leon Trotsky, telegram Special Order to the War Council of the 9th Army, November 1918. Quoted in Dmitri Volkogonov, *Trotsky: The Eternal Revolutionary*, Harper Collins, 1996, p.156.

"Do not look in the file of incriminating evidence to see whether or not the accused rose up against the Soviets with arms or words. Ask him instead to which class he belongs, what is his background, his education, his profession. These are the questions that will determine the fate of the accused. That is the meaning and essence of the Red Terror."

– Martin Latsis, Head of Ukrainian Cheka, in *Red Terror* newspaper, November 1918. Quoted in Yevgenia Albats, *The State Within a State: The KGB and Its Hold on Russia*, 1994.

"... catch and shoot the Astrakhan speculators and bribe-takers. These swine have to be dealt [with] so that everyone will remember it for years."

– V.I. Lenin, December 1918. Quoted in Dmitri Volkogonov, *Lenin: A New Biography* Free Press, 1994, p.201.

"When we are reproached with having established a dictatorship of one party... we say, 'Yes, it is a dictatorship of one party! This is what we stand for and we shall not shift from that position...'"

– V.I. Lenin, "Speech to the First All-Russia Congress of Workers in Education and Socialist Culture," *Pravda*, No.170, 5 August 1919.

"For us, there do not, and can not, exist the old systems of morality and 'humanity' invented by the bourgeoisie for the purpose of oppressing and exploiting the 'lower classes'. Our morality is new, our humanity is absolute, for it rests on the bright ideal of destroying all oppression and coercion. To us all is permitted, for we are the first in the world to raise the sword not in the name of enslaving and oppressing anyone, but in the name of freeing all from bondage ... Blood? Let there be blood, if it alone can turn the grey-white-and-black banner of the old piratical world to a scarlet hue, for only the complete and final death of that world will save us from the return of the old jackals."

– V.I. Lenin, in the first issue of *The Red Sword,* the weekly periodical of the Political Department of the Special Corps of Ukranian Cheka Troops, Kiev, 18 August 1919. Quoted in George Leggett, *The Cheka: Lenin's Political Police* , Oxford University Press, 1986, p.203.

"Treat the Jews (say it politely: Jewish petty bourgeoisie) and urban inhabitants in the Ukraine with an iron rod, transferring them to the front, not letting them into the government agencies (except in an insignificant percentage, in particu-

larly exceptional circumstances, under class control)."
– V.I. Lenin, "Draft Theses...Concerning Policy in the Ukraine",
Nov. 1919. Quoted in Richard Pipes, *The Unknown Lenin: From the Secret Archive*, 1996, p. 77.

"Russians are too kind, they lack the ability to apply determined methods of revolutionary terror."
– V.I. Lenin, August 1919. Quoted in Dmitri Volkogonov, *Lenin: A New Biography* Free Press, 1994, p.203.

"Everything is moral that promotes the victory of Communism".
– V.I. Lenin, from a lecture to Congress of Communist Youth, Moscow 1919. Quoted in Dmitri Volkogonov, *Lenin: A New Biography* Free Press, 1994, p.22.

"We have to run a hot iron down the spine of the Ukrainian kulaks – that will create a good working environment."
– Leon Trotsky, "Report to the Central Committee on Ukraine", c.1919. Quoted in Dmitri Volkogonov, *Trotsky: The Eternal Revolutionary*, Harper Collins, 1996, p.183.

"It is stupid to tolerate 'Nikola' [St. Nicholas, Santa Claus]; all Chekists have to be on alert to shoot anyone who doesn't turn up to work because of 'Nikola'."
– V.I. Lenin, 25 Dec. 1919. Quoted in Dmitri Volkogonov, *Autopsy for an Empire: The Seven Leaders who Built the Soviet Regime*, 1998, p.73-74.

1920-1929

"Not a single problem of the class struggle has ever been solved in history except by violence... The class struggle did not accidentally assume its latest form, in which the exploited class takes all the means of power in its own hands in order to completely destroy its class enemy, the bourgeoisie..."

– V.I. Lenin, "Part II: Report on the Activities of the Council of People's Commissars," Eighth All-Russia Congress of Soviets, 22 December 1920.

"As for us, we were never concerned with the Kantian-priestly and vegetarian-Quaker prattle about the 'sacredness of human life.'"
– Leon Trotsky, *Terrorism and Communism: A Reply to Karl Kautsky*, 1920. Retitled *Dictatorship Vs. Democracy*, Workers Party of America, 1922, p.63.

"[Communists, when necessary, must] resort to strategy and adroitness, illegal proceedings, reticence and subterfuge."
– V.I. Lenin, *The Infantile Sickness of Leftism*, 1920. Quoted in Dinko Tomasic, "Interrelations Between Bolshevik Ideology and the Structure of Soviet Society", *Am. Sociological Review,* 16(2), p.147. 1951.

"[Communists] must use any ruse, trick, veiling of truth... And to justify the use of any means in this struggle, the opponents of Bolshevism are pictured as being 'non-human' and are often referred to as 'gnats,' 'insects,' 'vermin,' 'reptiles,' 'dogs,' 'wild animals,' 'beasts of prey.' The principles of humanism are said not to apply to beasts."
– Dinko Tomasic, "Interrelations Between Bolshevik Ideology and the Structure of Soviet Society", Am. Sociological Review, 16(2), p.147, 1951, as taken from G.S. Counts and Nucia P. Lodge, *I Want to Be Like Stalin*, New York, 1948, p.72.

"The Red Terror is a weapon utilized against a class, doomed to destruction, which does not wish to perish... the Red Terror hastens the destruction of the bourgeoisie."
– Leon Trotsky, *Terrorism and Communism: A Reply to Karl Kautsky*, 1920. Retitled *Dictatorship Vs. Democracy*, Workers Party of America, 1922, p.64.

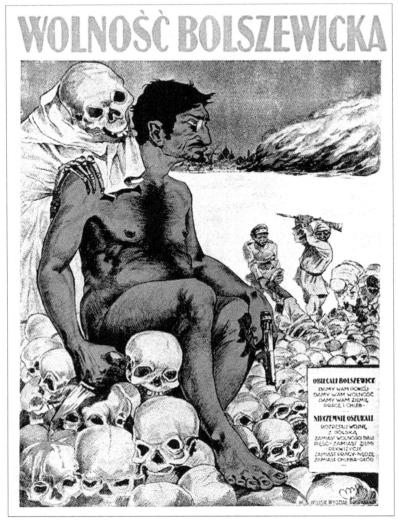

Polish poster decrying the bloody invasion of their homeland by the Red Army in 1920-1921, under the leadership of General Trotsky. Following on concepts of Marxist "War Communism", towards global conquest and formation of a world-wide International Communism, Lenin, Trotsky and Stalin viewed the conquest of Poland as a necessary spring-board for eventual conquest of Germany and the rest of Europe. They met fierce resistance from the Polish troops, however, who repulsed them back to the Soviet Union.

"... the road to socialism lies through a period of the highest possible intensification of the principle of the state. Just as a lamp, before going out, shoots up in a brilliant flame, so the state, before disappearing, assumes the form of the dictatorship of the proletariat, i.e., the most ruthless form of state, which embraces the life of the citizens authoritatively in every direction..."

– Leon Trotsky, *Terrorism and Communism: A Reply to Karl Kautsky*, 1920. Retitled *Dictatorship Vs. Democracy*, Workers Party of America, 1922, p.64.

"[We propose] the creation of a penal work command out of [work] deserters, and their internment in concentration camps. ... Repression for the attainment of economic ends is a necessary weapon of the socialist dictatorship."

– Leon Trotsky, *Terrorism and Communism: A Reply to Karl Kautsky*, 1920.

"... the very principle of labour conscription has replaced the principle of free labour as radically and irreversibly as socialization of the means of production has replaced capitalist ownership."

– Leon Trotsky, Speech at the April 1920 Trade Union Congress. Quoted in Dmitri Volkogonov, *Trotsky: The Eternal Revolutionary*, Harper Collins, 1996, p.216-7.

"[The Red Terror involves] terrorisation, arrests and the extermination of enemies of the revolution on the basis of their class affiliation or of their pre-revolutionary roles."

– Feliks Dzerzhinsky, head of Lenin's *Cheka* secret police, May 1920. Quoted in George Leggett, *The Cheka: Lenin's Political Police*, Clarendon Press, 1981, p.114.

"Do not believe that I seek revolutionary forms of justice. We don't need justice at this point... I propose, I demand, the

organization of revolutionary annihilation against all active counterrevolutionaries."

– Feliks Dzerzhinsky 1920. Quoted in Michel Heller and Aleksandr Nekrich, *Utopia in Power: A History of the USSR From 1917 to the Present* London: Hutchinson, 1986, p54.

"I am not fond of the Germans by any means but at the present time it is more advantageous to use them than to challenge them. An independent Poland is very dangerous to Soviet Russia: it is an evil which, however, at the present time has also its redeeming features; for while it exists, we may safely count on Germany, because the Germans hate Poland and will at any time make common cause with us in order to strangle Poland. ... Germany wants revenge, and we want revolution. For the moment our aims are the same. When our ways part they will be our most ferocious and our great enemies. Time will tell whether a German hegemony or a Communist federation is to arise out of the ruins of Europe."

– V.I. Lenin, "Speech to followers" *Ost-Information*, No.81, Berlin, 4 December 1920, Quoted in L.O. Dennis, *The Foreign Policies of Soviet Russia*, 1924, p.154.

"There is no point in proposing a benign program of pious wishes for peace without at the same time placing at the forefront the call for illegal organization and the summons to civil war."

– Leon Trotsky, *The Lessons of the Paris Commune*, February 1921. Quoted by Aleksandr Solzhenitsyn, *Warning to the West*, Farrar, Straus & Giroux, NY 1976.

"It is precisely now, and only now, when in the starving regions people are eating human flesh, and hundreds if not thousands of corpses are littering the roads, that we can (and therefore must) carry out the confiscation of church valuables with the most savage and merciless energy... to secure for ourselves a fund of several hundred million gold rubles... The

Soviet sailors at the Kronstadt fortress in Petrograd (St. Petersburg) who previously fought on behalf of Lenin's Bolshevik coup, finally realize his betrayal and openly called for an end to the Bolshevik dictatorship. "Soviets Without Communists" was their slogan, as they took over ships and the large naval fortress in Petrograd Bay. Trotsky, General of the Red Army, threatened them with annihilation unless they immediately surrendered. At the end of the battle, Trotsky's Red Army butchered both surrendered and wounded sailors, deporting survivors and their families to Siberia. Trotsky later evaded responsibility. The Kronstadt sailors were only the first of many groups who firstly supported Lenin's Bolshevik Communism and carried out various atrocities in its name, only later to disappear down the bowels of the very monster they helped to create.

greater the number of representatives of the reactionary clergy and reactionary bourgeoisie we succeed in executing for this reason, the better. We must teach these people a lesson right now, so that they will not dare even to think of any resistance for several decades."

– V.I. Lenin, letter to Molotov, 19 March 1922. Quoted in J.J. Wynot, *Keeping the Faith: Russian Orthodox Monasticism In the Soviet Union, 1917-1939*, Texas A&M Univ. Press, 2004, p.76; Also in Richard Pipes, *The Unknown Lenin: From the Secret Archive, 1996,* p. 152-4.

"By destroying the peasant economy and driving the peasant from the country to the town, the famine creates a proletariat... Furthermore the famine can and should be a progressive factor not only economically. It will force the peasant to reflect on the bases of the capitalist system, demolish faith in the tsar and tsarism, and consequently in due course make the victory of the revolution easier... Psychologically all this talk about feeding the starving and so on essentially reflects the usual sugary sentimentality of our intelligentsia."

– V.I. Lenin, c.1922. Quoted in Michael Ellman, "The Role of Leadership Perceptions and of Intent in the Soviet Famine of 1931-1934," *Europe-Asia Studies*, September 2005, p.823.

"Comrade Kursky! In my opinion we ought to extend the use of execution by shooting (allowing the substitution of exile abroad) to all activities of the Mensheviks, SR's, etc. We ought to find a formulation that would connect these activities with the international bourgeoisie."

– V.I. Lenin, to D.I. Kursky, May 1922. Quoted in Aleksandr Solzhenitsyn, *The Gulag Archipelago*, Harper & Row, 1973, p.353.

"Comrade Kursky! As a sequel to our conversation, I am sending you an outline of a supplementary paragraph for the Criminal Code... The basic concept, I hope, is clear, notwithstanding all the shortcomings of the rough draft: openly to set forth a statute which is both principled and politically truthful (and not just juridically narrow) to supply the motivation for the essence and the justification of terror, its necessity, its limits. The court must not exclude terror. It would be self-deception or deceit to promise this, and in order to provide it with a foundation and to legalize it. In a principled way, clearly and without hypocrisy and without embellishment, it is necessary to formulate it as broadly as possible, for only revolutionary righteousness and a revolutionary conscience will provide the conditions for applying it more or less broadly in practice.

With Communist greetings,
Lenin"

  – V.I. Lenin to D.I. Kursky, 17 May 1922. Quoted in Aleksandr Solzhenitsyn, *The Gulag Archipelago*, Harper & Row, 1973, p.353.

Hidden History of Communism's Founding Tyrants

Brief Timeline of
Early Communism

1818, May 5: Karl Marx is born, in Trier, Prussia of wealthy Jewish parents who had converted to Lutheranism a few years earlier, to avoid laws barring Jews from professional society. Marx was Baptized at age 6, but later became an atheist.

1820, Nov. 28: Friedrich Engels is born, in Barmen, Prussia, son of a wealthy Protestant factory owner whose fortunes supported him most of his life. He was later educated as a factory clerk and business apprentice, but gravitated towards revolutionary movements and atheism.

1835-36: Young Karl Marx attends the University of Bonn, Germany, but is shortly imprisoned and later expelled for drunkenness, disturbing the peace, indebtedness and dueling. He transfers to the University of Berlin to study Law and Philosophy. He joins a group of students devoted to Hegel's revolutionary ideas, critical of existing church and state institutions.

1838-1841: Engels works as apprentice in an import-export firm in Bremen, meanwhile cultivating a desire for revolution through his readings of Hegel. He becomes a militant atheist, writing revolutionary articles under the pseud. of "Friedrich Oswald".

1841: Marx graduates from the University, but his radicalism blocs him from regular employment. In Berlin, he writes as journalist for the liberal newspaper *Rheinische Zeitung*, becoming Editor one year later.

1842: Engels moves to London after a one-year stint as artillery officer in the Prussian military. He is converted now to Communism, writes inflammatory articles under pseudonym, and soon meets Marx on a visit to Paris.

1843-44: The Prussian government bans the *Rheinische Zeitung* for its radical writings. Marx resigns as editor, marries Jenny von Westphalen, from a wealthy upper-class family, and moves to Paris. There he helps found a radical journal *Deutsch-Französische Jahrbücher*, and meets Friedrich Engels. Marx is soon expelled from France for his writings, and travels to Belgium, where he founds another radical newspaper *Vorwärts!* Marx by then has abandoned Hegelism for Socialism and Communism.

1846-47: In Belgium, Marx founds the *Communist Correspondence Committee*. The London branch of the *New Communist League* asks Marx and Engels to write a *Manifesto of the Communist Party*.

1848: Marx/Engels publish the *Communist Manifesto*, and establish the journal *Neue Rheinische Zeitung*, with Marx as Editor-in-Chief. They are expelled from Belgium and move to London, where Marx joins with the *Communist League* and founds the *German Worker's Educational Society*.

1852-1862: Marx writes a series of articles promoting his Communism through the *New York Daily Tribune*. Marx personally remains destitute, living off his wife, Engels, and other donors.

1864: Marx helps found the *International Workingman's Association*, later termed the "First International", giving the inaugural address.

1867: Marx writes the first edition and volume of *Das Kapital*. The larger work as known today was edited and published only posthumously by Engels.

1869: Marx-inspired Sergey Nechayev, assisted by Mikhail Bakunin and others, promotes violent revolution in Russia. Revolutionaries such as Nechayev, influenced by Marx and Engels, call for a "merciless destruction" of society and state. "The ends justify the means", Nechayev declares, and "Everything that helps the revolution is moral. Everything that hinders it is immoral and criminal." Nechayev's writings, along with those of Marx and Engels, have a strong influence years later on Lenin, Stalin, Mao and other Communists.

1870, April 22: Vladimir Ilyich Ulyanov (after 1902: Lenin) is born and baptized in St. Petersburg, Russia, later converting to atheism.

Timeline of Communism

1871, March-May: A violent uprising takes place in Paris, with formation of the *Paris Commune,* a revolt against the state which is suppressed by the French central government. The exceptional violence within the Commune excites Marx and Engels.

1879, Nov. 7: Lev Davidovich Bronshtein is born in Bereslavka, Ukraine, Russia, of prosperous Jewish farmers. Bronshtein takes the name "Trotsky" in 1902, by which time he has also become an atheist.

1881: Russian Revolutionary terrorists assassinate Tsar Alexander II.

1883, March 14: Karl Marx dies of pleurisy in London.

1887: Ulyanov's (Lenin's) older brother Alexander is arrested in March and hanged in May for a bombing plot to kill Tsar Alexander III. Ulyanov (Lenin) is expelled from Kazan University in December, for taking part in student protests.

1889: Ulyanov (Lenin) enthusiastically reads Marx' *Das Kapital,* his first contact with Marxism.

1894: Ulyanov (Lenin) writes his first Marxist essay.

1895: Ulyanov (Lenin) travels through France, Germany and Switzerland to meet various Marxist revolutionaries, including the Russian revolutionary Plekhanov. Upon return he starts a Marxist newspaper, and is arrested.

1895, Aug. 5: Friedrich Engels dies in London.

1896: Ulyanov (Lenin) spends a year in prison, followed by unrestrained exile to Siberia for 3 years, where he marries and spends his time taking long walks, writing, hunting and swimming.

1896-97: Bronshtein (Trotsky) studies Marxism while at school in Odessa, helping to form the *South Russian Workers' Union.*

1898-1902: Bronshtein (Trotsky) is arrested for anti-Tsarist activities and sent to prison, followed by another sentence to Siberian exile.

Hidden History of Communism's Founding Tyrants

While in Siberia he meets and marries Alexandra Lvovna, another revolutionary, and has two daughters with her.

1900: Ulyanov (Lenin) leaves Russia for greater freedom in Europe, where he continues his contacts with Marxist leaders and factions.

1902: Ulyanov adopts the pseudonym "Lenin", or Vladimir Ilyich Lenin.

1902: Escaping from Siberia, Bronshtein changes his name to "Leon Trotsky". He abandons his wife and daughters in Siberia, escaping to London where he meets Lenin.

1905-1906: An early Russian Revolution is suppressed by Tsarist forces. Lenin and Trotsky temporarily return to Russia as participants, but are forced to flee again to Western Europe, where they continue with Communist activities and writings. To stave off discontent, the Tsar creates the first State Duma (Parliament).

1914, Aug.: World War 1 begins, with Tsarist Russia allied with the British, French and Italians, against the Kaiser's German Empire, allied with the Austro-Hungarian Empire and Ottoman Muslim Caliphate. Every political power in Russia supports the war effort against Germany except for Lenin's Bolsheviks, who accept secret financial aid from Germany.

1917, Feb-March: Revolution begins in Russia amid military defeats, desertions, food shortages and rampant economic inflation. The Russian Provisional Government is formed as the Romanov Tsar Nicholas II abdicates.

1917: Lenin arrives in St. Petersburg, on a special secret train car, organized for the trip by the German High Command. He is carrying weapons and massive German gold payments in a secret arrangement to foment revolution and pull Russia out of the war. The Bolshevik Red Guards are formed. Trotsky returns from New York. Lenin initially speaks in favor of democracy within the elected Russian Constituent Assembly, formed by the Russian Provisional Government of Kerensky. Lenin's Bolsheviks win only 25% of the seats. Lenin then changes to oppose democracy, and by disruptive militant actions with armed troops, takes over the Assembly and later banishes it. Shortly afterwards, all political parties except for the Bolsheviks are abolished, and newspapers are strictly censored. By November, Lenin, Trotsky and the Bolshevik Red Guards have routed the Russian Provisional Government of Kerensky, a reformist democrat, through corrosive scheming, arrests, assassinations and an armed coup. Lenin's Bolsheviks quickly abolish private land ownership, seizing all private resources, banks, factory works, etc., and begin truce talks with Germany, fulfilling his treasonous secret arrangement.

1917, Nov. 22: A preliminary armistice is signed by Germany and Russia, assisting Germany's new offensive against the Western Powers.

1917, Dec.: The *Cheka*, a political police force, is formed by Lenin ("The All-Russian Extraordinary Commission for Combating Counter-Revolution and Sabotage").

1917, Dec.: Soviet-German armistice talks take place at Brest-Litovsk. Lenin has already agreed to make great concessions to Germany, giving them huge territories in Finland, Ukraine and the three Baltic states, as secret payback for German help in transporting his Bolshevik group into Russia, and financing their *coup d'état* against the original pro-democratic February Russian Revolution. The *Treaty of Brest-Litovsk* is signed between Germany and the USSR on March 3rd of 1918, represented in the negotiations by Trotsky. Hostilities end as Russian lands are ceded to Germany. German troops once fighting Russians on the Eastern Front now are quickly transported to fight against the French, British and Americans on the Western Front.

1918-1921: Russian people revolt against Bolshevist dictatorship. Ukraine, Finland, Estonia, Latvia, Lithuania, Georgia, Armenia and Azerbaijan declare independence from the new Soviet dictatorship. The Don Cossacks revolt. General Trotsky leads a scorched-earth campaign against rebellious regions, with massacres of civilians. Millions of peasants are starved as the Red Army confiscates grain to feed urban regions under economic collapse. "War Communism" policies are introduced, with the entire Soviet economy subordinated to

Hidden History of Communism's Founding Tyrants

state controls, alongside the utopian "necessity" to spread Communism violently over the entire world, so that free people and capital have no place to flee to, or hide. Border controls are instituted to prevent anyone from entering or departing the Soviet Union without official permissions. Total control of print media is instituted. (Radio and TV media do not yet exist).

1918, Spring: British and French land small expeditionary forces at Murmansk, Archangel and Vladivostock, with the goal of supporting anti-Bolshevik forces, restoring the Eastern Front against Germany, and to block German and allied Finnish troops from building a submarine base. Anti-Bolshevik Russians cannot rally sufficient support for the British-French effort, and the expeditionary force retreats.

1918, June 16: Lenin officially reinstates the death penalty, expanding it to target entire groups based upon social class or ideology, and refusing accused parties the rights to call their own witnesses. Executions exceed anything seen during Tsarist times.

1918, July 17: Tsar Nicholas II and his family are executed on orders from Lenin.

1918, Aug. 30: Assassination of Petrograd Cheka leader Moisei Uritsky by Leonid Kannegisser. Attempted assassination of Lenin by Fanni Kaplan.

1918, Sept.-Oct.: The Soviet newspaper *Izvestiya* publishes "Appeal to the Working Class", the first official announcement of the Red Terror. The Cheka issues a decree "On Red Terror". Mass arrests begin. Tens of thousands of oppositionists are rounded up and promptly executed without trials, including previously arrested persons held in prisons.

1918, Oct. 28: Austria-Hungary sues for peace, to end their participation in WW1.

1918, Nov. 11: Germany is defeated on the battlefield, and WW1 is ended. The Soviet Government promptly renounces the Treaty of Brest-Litovsk and reclaims lands previously ceded to Germany.

Timeline of Communism

1919, April: First Gulag Concentration Camps are developed in Soviet Russia, under Lenin's leadership.

1920, April-May: Polish-Soviet War. The Red Army under General Trotsky is repulsed from Poland.

1921: The Soviet Communist economy is devastated, prompting Lenin's New Economic Policy, allowing small-scale capitalism to supply basic commodities and food. In May, the Kronstadt Sailors at Petrograd revolt against the Bolshevik dictatorship, calling for "Soviets without Communists". They are routed by the Red Army under command of General Trotsky, who orders execution of surrendered sailors, allowing his Army to loot and commit atrocities against their family members and civilians. He later denies responsibility.

1922, April: Josef Stalin becomes General Secretary of the Communist Party. Germany formally recognizes the Soviet Union.

1922, May 26: Lenin suffers his first stroke, with the second in December, and a third the following March 1923, after which he can no longer speak. He is disabled, and dies less than two years later.

1924, Jan. 21: Lenin dies and Stalin ascends to full power. A new Soviet Constitution is founded upon "dictatorship of the proletariat" and abolition of private property in land and the means of production.

1928, Jan.11: Trotsky is banished by Stalin to internal exile in Alma-Ata, Soviet Central Asia. Stalin is now in full command of the Soviet Union.

1928: Collectivization of Soviet agriculture begins as millions of "Kulaks", owners of productive family farms, and other dissenters are rounded up and shot, or deported to the Gulag, their land and property looted by the Red Army commissars. The first "Five Year Plan" is instituted, leading to further economic destitution, and repressive Communist rule.

1929, Feb.: Trotsky is deported from the USSR by Stalin. Trotsky then begins writing a series of books which white-wash Bolshevik crimes, and his own involvement in them. "Trotsky the moderate humanitarian" emerges to Western audiences, as the defeated "rational alternative" to Stalin. Stalin cannot reveal too much about Trotsky's barbaric murdering of civilians and surrendered soldiers, etc., during Lenin's time, as it would soil the white-washed reputation of the murdering Lenin. Also at risk are on-going secret Soviet-German cooperations, since the end of WW1, for undermining the Treaty of Versailles disarmament clauses, forbidding Germany to rebuild its military. Lenin, Trotsky and Stalin had all been involved in secret plans for German technicians and engineers to build new munitions factories deep in Soviet territory, away from the prying eyes of the Versailles inspectors, with a sharing of produced armaments. New generations of fighter and bomber aircraft, tanks and artillery, poison gas and other weapons were secretly manufactured and tested in these new factories, in joint plans between the Soviets and German High Command, towards a later open war of conquest against the rest of the world. This deception remained secret even after 1933, when Hitler rose to power, and massive quantities of every kind of new and frightening weaponry appeared in Germany "as if by magic". The better-known "Hitler-Stalin Pact" of 1939, just before the joint invasion of Poland by Germany and the Soviet Union, was the first public announcement of a deadly plot for world conquest, hatched between the German militarists and the Bolshevist Soviets almost two decades earlier.

1936-38: Thousands are purged from the Soviet government and military as real or alleged followers of Trotsky. Nearly all are given death-sentences or sent off to disappear in the Soviet Gulag slave-labor death-camps, which have greatly expanded by this time.

1939, Aug. 23: A non-aggression pact is signed between Nazi Germany and the Soviet Union, the "Molotov-Ribbentrop Pact", or "Hitler-Stalin Pact". Hidden side-agreements divide up Europe for mutual conquest.

1939, Sept. 1: World War 2 begins. Nazi Germany invades Western Poland; shortly thereafter, the Soviet Union invades Eastern Poland, Finland, Latvia, Lithuania and Estonia.

1940, Aug. 21: Trotsky is assassinated by Stalin's agents in Mexico City.

Recommended Readings
On Communism and Marxism
Historical and Contemporary

Albats, Yevgenia: *The State Within a State: The KGB and Its Hold on Russia*, Farrar, Straus and Giroux, 1994.

Andrew, Christopher & Vasili Mitrokhin: *The Sword and the Shield: Secret History of the KGB*, Basic Books, 1999.

Antonov-Ovseyenko, Anton: *Portrait of a Tyrant* (Russian), 1981.

Barron, John & Anthony Paul, *Peace With Horror: The Untold Story of Communist Genocide in Cambodia.* Hodder & Stoughton,1977.

Bazhanov, Boris: *Bazhanov & Damnation Of Stalin*, Ohio U. Press 1990.

Beal, Fred: *Proletarian Journey*, Hillman-Curl, 1937.

Burns, E. (Ed.): *A Handbook of Marxism*, 1935.

Catino, Martin S.: *The Aggressors: Ho Chi Minh, North Vietnam and the Communist Bloc*, Dog Ear Publishing, 2010.

Chang, Jung & Jon Halliday, *Mao: The Unknown Story*, Jonathan Cape, 2005.

Conquest, Robert: *Reflections on a Ravaged Century*, Norton, 2000.

Conquest, Robert: *The Harvest of Sorrow: Soviet Collectivization and the Terror-Famine*, Oxford Univ. Press, 1987.

Courtois, Stephan, et al.: *The Black Book of Communism: Crimes, Terror, Repression*, Harvard U. Press, 1999.

Crossman, Richard, Editor: *The God That Failed*, Bantam Books, 1965..

Dallin, Alexander & George Breslauer: *Political Terror in Communist Systems,* Stanford U. Press, 1970.

Dennis, L.O.: *The Foreign Policies of Soviet Russia*, 1924.

Dikötter, Frank: *Mao's Great Famine; The Story of China's Most Devastating Catastrophe,* Bloomsbury, 2010.

Dilas, Milovan: *Conversations with Stalin*, Harcourt, Brace & World, 1962.

Duncanson, Dennis: *Government and Revolution in Vietnam*, Oxford U. Press, 1968.

Hidden History of Communism's Founding Tyrants

Fontova, Humberto: *Fidel: Hollywood's Favorite Tyrant*, Regnery 2005.

Fontova, Humberto: *Exposing the Real Che Guevara, and the Useful Idiots who Idolize Him*, Penguin, 2007.

Gellately, Robert: *Lenin, Stalin and Hitler: The Age of Scial Catastrophe*, Robert Knopf, 2007.

Ghosh, Palash: "How Many People Did Joseph Stalin Kill?", *Int. Business Times*, 5 March 2013, Internet article.

Gregory, Paul R.: *Terror by Quota: State Security from Lenin to Stalin*, Yale U. Press, 2009.

Hao, Tran Manh: "50 Years On, Vietnamese Remember Land Reform Terror". 2006, Internet article.

Haynes, John E. & Harvey Klehr: *In Denial: Historians, Communism & Espionage*, Encounter Books, 2003.

Heller, Michael & Aleksandr Nekrich: *Utopia in Power: A History of the USSR From 1917 to the Present* London: Hutchinson, 1986.

Hubbell, John G.: "The Blood-Red Hands of Ho Chi Minh", *Readers Digest*, Nov. 1968.

Kravchenko, Victor: *I Chose Freedom*, Transaction Publishers, 1989.

Leggett, George: *The Cheka: Lenin's Political Police*, Clarendon Press, 1981.

Lind, Michael: *Vietnam: The Necessary War*, Free Press 1999.

Luckett, Richard: *The White Generals: An Account of the White Movement and the Russian Civil War*, Viking Press, 1971.

Medvedev, Roy: *Let History Judge*, Columbia U. Press, 1989.

Melgunov, S.P.: *Bolshevik Seizure of Power*, 1939, reprinted ABC-Clio Press, 1972.

Melgunov, S.P.: *The Red Terror in Russia*, Hyperion 1975.

Meyer, Arno: *The Furies: Violence and Terror in the French and Russian Revolutions*, Princeton U. Press, 2002.

Miliukov, Paul: *Russia and Its Crisis*, 1905, reprinted Barnes & Nobel, 2005.

Miliukov, Paul: *The Russian Revolution, Vol.3: Reforms, Reactions, Revolutions (1855-1932)*, Funk & Wagnalls, 1969..

Miliukov, Paul: *Political Memoirs 1905-1917*, U. of Michigan Press, 1967.

Muggeridge, Malcolm: "War on the Peasants", *Fortnightly Review*, XXXIX, May 1933

Recommended Reading

Nixon, Richard: *No More Vietnams*, Arbor House 1985.

Pike, Douglas: *The Viet Cong Strategy of Terror*, monograph, 1970.

Pipes, Richard: *The Unknown Lenin: From the Secret Archive*, Yale Univ. Press, 1998

Radzinsky, Edward: *Stalin: The First In-depth Biography Based on Explosive New Documents from Russia's Secret Archives*, Anchor, 1997.

Schmehl, Paul: "The Hue Massacre: A Study of Communist Policies and Tactics in Vietnam", *Vietnam Veterans for Factual History*, 24 Jan 2015, Internet article.

Service, Robert: *Stalin: A Biography*, Macmillan 2004.

Shifrin, Avraham: *Guidebook to Prisons and Concentration Camps of the Soviet Union*, Bantam, 1987

Sokolov, B.: *Truth About the Great Patriotic War* (Russian), 1998.

Solzhenitsyn, Aleksandr: *The Gulag Archipelago*, Harper & Row, 1973.

Solzhenitsyn, Aleksandr: *Warning to the West*, Farrar, Straus & Giroux, NY 1976.

Solzhenitsyn, Aleksandr: "A World Split Apart", Commencement address to Harvard University, 8 June 1978.

Sorokin, Pitirim: *Leaves from a Russian Diary*, Beacon Press, Boston 1950.

Taylor, S.J.: *Stalin's Apologist: Walter Duranty, the New York Times Man in Moscow*, Oxford U. Press, 1990.

Tomasic, Dinko: "Interrelations Between Bolshevik Ideology and the Structure of Soviet Society", *Am. Sociological Review*, 16(2),. 1951.

Tuong, Nguyen Ly: "Massacre at Hue, in my Eyes", *Mau Than*, 8 March 2009, Internet article.

US Senate Subcommittee on *Strategy and Tactics of World Communism*, May 1954.

US Senate Intelligence Report: *The Human Cost of Communism in Vietnam*, 1972.

Vennema, Alje: *The Viet Cong Massacre at Hue*, Vantage Press, 1976.

Volkogonov, Dmitri: *Autopsy for an Empire: The Seven Leaders who Built the Soviet Regime*, 1998.

Volkogonov, Dmitri: *Lenin: A New Biography* Free Press, 1994.

Volkogonov, Dmitri: *Trotsky: The Eternal Revolutionary*, Harper Collins, 1996.

Weyl, Nathanial: *Karl Marx: Racist,* Arlington House, 1979.
Wu, Harry: *Laogai: The Chinese Gulag,* Westview Press, 1992.
Wu, Harry: "The Other Gulag", *National Review*, 4/5/1999, Vol.51, No.6.
Zhisui, Li: *The Private Life of Chairman Mao,* Random House, 1994.

On Secret German-Soviet Military Alliances and Armaments Factories, 1919 through 1941.

Albrecht, Ulrich: *The Soviet Armaments Industry*, Harwood Academic Pub., 1993, p.13-17, 57, 62-67.
Ericson, Edward E.: *Feeding the German Eagle: Soviet Economic Aid to Nazi Germany*, Praeger, 1999.
Freund, Gerald: *Unholy Alliance: Russian German Relations from the Treaty of Brest-Litovsk to the Treaty of Berlin*, Harcourt Brace & Co., 1957.
Gatzk, Hans W.: *Stresemann and the Rearmament of Germany*, Johns Hopkins Press, 1954.
Suvorov, Viktor: *The Chief Culprit: Stalin's Grand Design to Start World War II,* Naval Institute Press, Annapolis, 2008, p.17-18.
Vourkoutiotis, Vasilis: *Making Common Cause: German-Soviet Secret Relations*, 1919-1922, Palgrave-Macmillan, 2007.

Recommended Reading

Internet Resources:

Items by Marx, Engels, Lenin, Trotsky and other Communists
(Caution: Many inflammatory items deleted to conceal the racist
and genocidal ambitions of Communist leaders.)
www.marxists.org
www.marxists.org/archive/marx/letters/
www.marxists.org/archive/marx/works/subject/
newspapers/neue-rheinische-zeitung.htm
www.marxists.org/archive/marx/works/subject/
newspapers/new-york-tribune.htm

Discover the Networks Website
www.discoverthenetworks.org/

Marx & Friends In their Own Words
marxwords.blogspot.com/

Never Blame the Left
jonjayray.tripod.com/watson.html

Hitler Was a (Nationalist) Socialist
democraticpeace.wordpress.com/2009/05/23/hitler-was-a-
socialist/

R.J. Rummell's Website on Democide
www.hawaii.edu/powerkills/welcome.html

Paul Bogandor's Website on Leftism
www.paulbogdanor.com/writings.html

Vietnam Veterans for Factual History
blog.vvfh.org/

Fighting the Lost (Vietnam) War
vnafmamn.com/fighting_lostwar.html

About the Author

James DeMeo, PhD, formally studied the Earth, Atmospheric, and Environmental Sciences at Florida International University and the University of Kansas, where he earned a Doctorate in Geography in 1986. DeMeo has undertaken social, physical-geographical and atmospheric research in the arid American Southwest, Egypt, Israel, sub-Saharan Africa, and Namibia, Africa. His work on the *Saharasian* "Origins of Violence" question[§] produced the largest global cross-cultural study to date, on the subjects of family, sexual life, and the development of repressive social institutions. His social, geographical and historical research uncovered how extreme *hyperarid desert climates of famine* can force entire societies towards child-abusing, sadomasochistic and sex-repressive behaviors, with emergent totalitarian state structures. His work on the *Genocide Quotes* was a product of that line of study, a line that included work with new experimental approaches for desert-greening.

DeMeo's published works include dozens of articles and compendiums, with many books and edited volumes. DeMeo served on the Faculties of Geography (Earth and Atmospheric Sciences) at the University of Kansas, Illinois State University, University of Miami and University of Northern Iowa. In 1989, he retired from academic teaching to enter private research. DeMeo's primary books are listed on the front page of this work, and are available through most on-line bookstores. A list of his major scientific publications is given at Academia.edu:

https://orgonelab.academia.edu/JamesDeMeo

[§] James DeMeo, *Saharasia: the 4000 BCE Origins of Child-Abuse, Sex-Repression, Warfare and Social Violence, In the Deserts of the Old World,* Natural Energy Works, 1996, 2006.

CPSIA information can be obtained
at www.ICGtesting.com
Printed in the USA
LVHW040732280819
629229LV00017B/932

9 780997 405705